A Kangaroo Mob /
Una manada de canguros

By Johanna Burke

Traducción al español: Eduardo Alamán

Gareth Stevens
Publishing

Please visit our website, www.garethstevens.com. For a free color catalog of all our high-quality books, call toll free 1-800-542-2595 or fax 1-877-542-2596.

Library of Congress Cataloging-in-Publication Data

Burke, Johanna
[A kangaroo mob. Spanish & English]
A kangaroo mob = Una manada de canguros / by Johanna Burke ; traducción al español, Eduardo Alamán.
          p.   cm. – (Animal groups = Grupos de animales)
Includes bibliographical references and index.
Contents: Life in the mob = Vida en la manada — Kinds of kangaroos = Tipos de canguros — Mob members = Miembros de la manada — Roo range = Praderas de canguros — Safety in the mob = Seguridad en la manada — Talking with kangaroos = Hablando con los canguros - Growing up = Creciendo — Adult kangaroos = Canguros adultos — Boxing boomers = Boxeadores.
ISBN 978-1-4339-8804-2 (hardcover)
1. Kangaroos—Juvenile literature   2. Social behavior in animals—Juvenile literature   [1. Kangaroos 2. Social behavior in animals   3. Spanish language materials—Bilingual]   I. Alamán, Eduardo   II. Title   III. Title: Manada de canguros 2013
          599.2/2—dc23

First Edition

Published in 2013 by
Gareth Stevens Publishing
111 East 14th Street, Suite 349
New York, NY 10003

Designer: Ben Gardner
Editor: Greg Roza

Photo credits: Cover, p. 1 © iStockphoto.com/Craig Dingle; interior backgrounds Daniiel/Shutterstock.com; p. 5 Tier Und Naturfotographie J and C Sohns/Photographer's Choice/Getty Images; p. 7 (red kangaroo) Vladimir Wrangel/Shutterstock.com; p. 7 (gray kangaroo) Kitch Bain/Shutterstock.com; p. 7 (tree kangaroo) Daniel J Cox/Oxford Scientific/Getty Images; p. 9 Julie Lucht/Shutterstock.com; p. 11 Natalia Lysenko/Shutterstock.com; p. 13 Martin Mette/Shutterstock.com; p. 15 dmvphotos/ Shutterstock.com; p. 17 markrhiggins/Shutterstock.com; p. 19 Jin Young Lee/ Shutterstock.com; p. 20 Sweetheart/Shutterstock.com; p. 21 Janelle Lugge/Shutterstock.com.

Printed in the United States of America

CPSIA compliance information: Batch #CW13GS: For further information contact Gareth Stevens, New York, New York at 1-800-542-2595.

Contents

Contenido

Life in the Mob

Kangaroos are furry animals that live mostly in Australia. They have big ears. They have large back feet, and they're very good hoppers! Kangaroos live in groups called mobs. There can be more than 50 kangaroos in a mob.

Vida en la manada

Los canguros son animales peludos que viven principalmente en Australia. Los canguros tienen orejas grandes. También tienen patas traseras grandes y son muy buenos saltando. Los canguros viven en grupos llamados manadas. Una manada puede tener más de 50 canguros.

Kinds of Kangaroos

There are many kinds of kangaroos. Red kangaroos are the largest kind. They can be as tall as an adult person. Gray kangaroos are the most common kind. Tree kangaroos live in trees! All kinds live in mobs.

Tipos de canguros

Hay muchos tipos de canguros. Los canguros rojos son los más grandes. Pueden ser tan altos como una persona adulta. Los canguros grises son los más comunes. ¡Los canguros arborícolas viven en árboles! Todos los canguros viven en manadas.

red kangaroo/
canguro rojo

gray kangaroo/
canguro gris

tree kangaroo/
canguro arborícola

7

Mob Members

Male kangaroos are called boomers. A mob has one male leader. Sometimes other males live in a mob, too. Females are called flyers. They care for young kangaroos. Young kangaroos are called joeys. Joeys love to play.

Miembros de la manada

Los canguros machos son los líderes de la manada. Cada manada tiene un líder. En ocasiones, otros machos viven en la manada. Las hembras se encargan de los canguros jóvenes. A los canguros jóvenes les encanta jugar.

9

Roo Range

Kangaroos eat at night and rest during the day. They eat grass and leaves. Kangaroos drink water whenever they can find it. A mob will travel far away from their home **range** to find food, but they often come back.

- -

Praderas de canguros

Los canguros comen por la noche y descansan durante el día. Los canguros comen hierba y hojas. Los canguros beben agua en donde la encuentran. Una manada puede viajar fuera de su **pradera** en busca de comida, pero generalmente regresa a su pradera.

11

Safety in the Mob

Mobs keep kangaroos safe. Some kangaroos watch for enemies, such as **dingoes**, while the others eat or sleep. When an enemy is near, a kangaroo stomps its feet. This warns the rest of the mob of **danger**.

Seguridad en la manada

La manada mantiene a los canguros seguros. Algunos canguros de la manada alertan sobre sus enemigos como los dingos, mientras el resto de la manada duerme o se alimenta. Cuando se acerca un enemigo, los canguros pisan fuerte con sus patas. Esto le avisa al resto de la manada sobre el peligro.

13

Talking with Kangaroos

The kangaroos in a mob **communicate** in many ways. They grunt, cough, and hiss. They growl when they're mad. Mothers make a clicking sound to call their joeys. Kangaroos also **groom** new mob members to learn about them.

- -

Hablando con los canguros

Los canguros de una manada **se comunican** de varias formas. Los canguros gruñen, silban o tosen. Los canguros gruñen cuando se enojan. Las mamás hacen un chasquido para llamar a sus crias. Además, los canguros reconocen a los nuevos miembros de la manada tocando su piel.

Growing Up

Female kangaroos have pouches. This is where newborn joeys live. As a joey gets bigger, it climbs in and out of the pouch. A mother often has a joey in her pouch and an older joey by her side.

- -

Creciendo

Las hembras de los canguros tienen bolsas donde guardan a los canguros recién nacidos. Cuando el canguro crece, sale de la bolsa. Con frecuencia una mamá canguro tiene un recién nacido en su bolsa y un canguro joven a su lado.

Adult Kangaroos

Female kangaroos often stay with their mothers even after they have their own joeys. When boomers grow up, they might leave the mob to join a new one. Or they might start a mob of their own.

Canguros adultos

Con frecuencia, las hembras se quedan con sus mamás aunque hayan tenido sus propios cachorros. Cuando los jóvenes machos crecen pueden dejar su manada para unirse a otra. También pueden formar su propia manada.

19

Boxing Boomers

Kangaroos love living in a mob. They get along most of the time. When boomers get angry, they "box." They kick each other with their feet. Joeys and flyers box, too. But they're just having fun!

Boxeadores

A los canguros les gusta vivir en la manada. Pero, cuando los jóvenes macho se enojan comienzan a "boxear". Se golpean entre ellos con sus patas. ¡Los más jovenes también lo hacen, pero solo como diversion!

Fun Facts About Kangaroos/ Datos divertidos sobre los canguros

Kangaroos can't walk backwards, but they're very good swimmers.

Los canguros no pueden caminar hacia atrás, pero son muy buenos nadadores.

Depending on the kind, kangaroos can live between 7 and 18 years.

Según la clase, algunos canguros pueden vivir entre 7 y 18 años.

The smallest kangaroo is the musky rat kangaroo. It's only about 8 inches (20 cm) tall.

El canguro rata almizclado es el más pequeño del mundo. Solo mide 8 pulgadas (20 cm) de altura.

Red kangaroos can cover 15 feet (4.6 m) with one hop!

¡Los canguro rojos pueden brincar hasta 15 pies (4.6 m) en un brinco!

Glossary

communicate: to share ideas and feelings through sounds and motions

danger: something that can cause harm

dingo: a wild Australian dog with a reddish-brown coat

groom: to clean

range: the area where something lives

Glosario

comunicarse: compartir ideas y sentimientos mediante sonidos o movimiento

dingo: un perro salvaje de Australia con pelaje rojo y marrón

peligro: algo que puede causar daño

pradera: el área en la que viven los canguros

For More Information/ Para más información

Books

Riggs, Kate. *Kangaroos.* Mankato, MN: Creative Education, 2012.

Robbins, Lynette. *Kangaroos.* New York, NY: PowerKids Press, 2012.

Wood, Jenny. *I Wonder Why Kangaroos Have Pouches.* Boston, MA: Kingfisher, 2011.

Websites

Animal Bytes: Kangaroo and Wallaby
www.sandiegozoo.org/animalbytes/t-kangaroo.html
Learn more about kangaroos and their close cousins, wallabies.

Kangaroos
kids.nationalgeographic.com/kids/animals/creaturefeature/kangaroos
Read more about kangaroos and see pictures of them.

Index

Índice